Me and My Friends

I Can Share

written by Daniel Nunn

illustrated by Clare Elsom

Chicago, Illinois

© 2015 Heinemann Library,
an imprint of Capstone Global Library, LLC
Chicago, Illinois

All rights reserved. No part of this publication may be reproduced or transmitted in any form or by any means, electronic or mechanical, including photocopying, recording, taping, or any information storage and retrieval system, without permission in writing from the publisher.

Edited by Brynn Baker
Designed by Steve Mead and Kyle Grenz
Production by Helen McCreath
Original illustrations © Clare Elsom
Originated by Capstone Global Library Ltd

Library of Congress Cataloging-in-Publication Data
Cataloging-in-publication information is on file with the Library of Congress.

ISBN 978-1-4846-0247-8 (paperback)
ISBN 978-1-4846-0257-7 (ebook PDF)

Contents

Sharing................ 4
Sharing Quiz............ 20
Picture Glossary......... 22
Index................ 22
Notes for Teachers
and Parents............ 23
In this Book............ 24

Sharing

I **share** with my **friend**.

My friends share with me.

I share my games.

My friend shares with me.

I share my apple.

My friend shares with me.

I share my crayons.

My friends share with me.

I share my shovel.

My friend shares with me.

I share my books.

My friend shares with me.

I share my bike.

My friend shares with me.

I share with my friends.

We have fun when we share!

Sharing Quiz

Which of these pictures shows sharing?

Did sharing make these children happy? Why? Do you like to share?

Picture Glossary

friend person you care about and have fun with

share to divide equally or take turns

Index

apples 8
bikes 16
books 14

crayons 10
games 6
shovels 12

Notes for Teachers and Parents

BEFORE READING

Building background: Ask children what it means to share. Have them name some things they share with family members, classmates, and friends. Is it hard to share? Why or why not?

AFTER READING

Recall and reflection: Ask the class how children in the book had fun. (playing games, reading books) What do we need to do to be a good friend? (take turns, share)

Sentence knowledge: Ask children to find a capital letter and a period in the book. Ask what a capital letter and a period signify.

Word knowledge (phonics): Have children point to the word *share* on page 4. Sound out the three phonemes in the word *sh/a/re*. Ask children to sound out each phoneme as they point to the letters, and then blend the sounds together to make the word *share*. Can they think of other words that start with the sound *sh*? (shadow, shake, shout)

Word recognition: Have children count how many times *share/shares* appears in the main text (not counting the quiz). (16)

AFTER-READING ACTIVITIES

Place children in small groups to write and draw about something they share with friends. Give each child only one tool, such as crayons, scissors, pencils, and so on. Children will need to share the materials to complete the work.

In this Book

Topic
sharing

Topic Words
apple
bike
books
crayons
friend
games
share
shovel

Sentence Stems
I ____ with my ___.
My ___ shares with ___.
I ___ my ___.
We have ___ when we ___.

High-frequency Words
have
I
me
my
we
when
with